Table of Contents

Chapter 1: Introduction to AI-generated Disinformation 3
    The rise of AI-generated content 3
    Challenges posed by deepfakes 4
    Need for robust measures to detect and mitigate misinformation 5

Chapter 2: AI-generated Political Propaganda 6
    Impact on elections 6
    Strategies for detecting AI-generated political propaganda 7

Chapter 3: AI-generated Fake News 8
    Spread of fake news through AI 8
    Tools for identifying AI-generated fake news 9

Chapter 4: AI-generated Social Media Manipulation 10
    Techniques used for social media manipulation 10
    Countermeasures for combating AI-generated social media manipulation 11

Chapter 5: AI-generated Disinformation in Healthcare 12
    Threats posed by AI-generated disinformation in healthcare 12
    Approaches for addressing misinformation in the healthcare sector 13

Chapter 6: AI-generated Disinformation in Finance 15
    Impact of AI-generated disinformation on financial markets 15
    Steps for mitigating financial fraud through AI 16

Chapter 7: AI-generated Disinformation in Entertainment 17
    Influence of AI-generated content on the entertainment industry 17
    Strategies for identifying and combating misinformation in entertainment 18

Chapter 8: AI-generated Disinformation in Education 19
    Role of AI-generated content in education 19
    Measures for preventing the spread of misinformation in educational settings 20

Chapter 9: AI-generated Disinformation in Cybersecurity 21
    Threats of AI-generated disinformation in cybersecurity 21
    Best practices for protecting against AI-driven cyber attacks 22

Chapter 10: AI-generated Disinformation in Climate Change 23

    Impact of AI-generated misinformation on climate change discourse 23

    Initiatives for promoting accurate information on climate issues 24

Chapter 11: AI-generated Disinformation in International Relations 25

    Use of AI in spreading disinformation in global politics 25

    Diplomatic efforts to combat AI-generated misinformation on the international stage 26

Chapter 12: Conclusion and Future Outlook 27

    Summary of key points 27

    Recommendations for professionals in combating AI-generated misinformation 28

Chapter 1: Introduction to AI-generated Disinformation

The rise of AI-generated content

The rise of AI-generated content has become a significant concern in recent years, particularly in the context of elections. Deepfakes, which are highly realistic videos created using artificial intelligence, have the potential to spread misinformation and manipulate public opinion. This trend highlights the need for robust measures to detect and mitigate the spread of AI-generated disinformation in political campaigns.

AI-generated political propaganda is another growing concern, as it can be used to manipulate public perception of candidates and sway voter opinions. The use of AI in creating fake news articles and social media posts has become increasingly sophisticated, making it difficult for the average person to discern what is true and what is false. Professionals in the field of disinformation detection must stay vigilant in order to combat this threat to democracy.

In addition to political propaganda, AI-generated content is also being used to spread misinformation in other sectors such as healthcare, finance, entertainment, education, cybersecurity, climate change, and international relations. In the healthcare industry, for example, AI-generated disinformation can lead to dangerous misconceptions about treatments and prevention methods. In finance, AI can be used to manipulate stock prices and create false narratives about companies. The implications of AI-generated disinformation in these sectors are far-reaching and require immediate attention.

Professionals working in the field of disinformation detection must develop innovative strategies to combat the spread of AI-generated content. This may involve developing advanced algorithms to detect deepfakes, monitoring social media platforms for suspicious activity, and collaborating with experts in various industries to identify and debunk false information. By staying ahead of the curve and adapting to the changing landscape of AI-generated content, professionals can help protect society from the harmful effects of misinformation.

In conclusion, the rise of AI-generated content presents new challenges for professionals in the field of disinformation detection. From political propaganda to healthcare misinformation, the spread of AI-generated disinformation has the potential to cause serious harm to society. By developing robust measures to detect and mitigate the spread of false information, professionals can help safeguard the integrity of elections, protect public health, and ensure the reliability of information in various sectors. It is imperative that professionals in this field remain vigilant and proactive in their efforts to combat the spread of AI-generated content.

Challenges posed by deepfakes

Challenges posed by deepfakes are becoming increasingly prevalent in today's digital landscape. Deepfakes, which are AI-generated videos that manipulate or fabricate content to make it appear genuine, present a significant threat to the spread of misinformation. In the context of elections, deepfakes can be used to create false narratives about political candidates, sway public opinion, and undermine the democratic process. Detecting and mitigating deepfakes is crucial to preserving the integrity of elections and ensuring that voters have access to accurate information.

One of the main challenges posed by deepfakes is the difficulty in distinguishing between genuine and manipulated content. Deepfake technology has become increasingly sophisticated, making it harder for individuals to discern what is real and what is fake. This can lead to the rapid spread of false information, as deepfakes are often shared widely on social media platforms before they can be debunked. As a result, deepfakes have the potential to cause widespread confusion and distrust among the public, making it more challenging to combat the spread of misinformation.

Another challenge posed by deepfakes is their potential to be used as a tool for political propaganda. By creating fake videos of political figures saying or doing things they never actually did, deepfakes can be used to manipulate public perception and influence election outcomes. This type of AI-generated disinformation poses a serious threat to the democratic process, as it can undermine the credibility of political candidates and erode trust in the electoral system. Detecting and mitigating deepfakes in the context of political propaganda is essential to safeguarding the integrity of elections and ensuring that voters are not misled by false information.

In addition to political propaganda, deepfakes are also being used to spread fake news and manipulate social media platforms. AI-generated fake news articles and videos can be used to deceive the public, promote harmful ideologies, and sow discord among communities. Similarly, AI-generated social media manipulation tactics, such as creating fake accounts or using bots to amplify false information, can be used to manipulate public opinion and undermine trust in legitimate sources of information. Detecting and mitigating deepfakes in the context of fake news and social media manipulation is critical to combating the spread of misinformation and ensuring that individuals have access to accurate and reliable information.

Overall, the rise of deepfakes poses a range of challenges that must be addressed in order to protect individuals from the harmful effects of AI-generated misinformation. From political propaganda to fake news and social media manipulation, deepfakes have the potential to disrupt democratic processes, erode trust in institutions, and undermine public discourse. Detecting and mitigating deepfakes is essential for professionals working in a variety of fields, including politics, journalism, cybersecurity, and beyond, to ensure that accurate and reliable information remains accessible to all. By developing robust measures to combat the spread of deepfakes, professionals can help safeguard the integrity of elections, protect the public from misinformation, and uphold the principles of truth and transparency in the digital age.

Need for robust measures to detect and mitigate misinformation

In today's digital age, the rise of AI-generated content, including deepfakes, is posing new challenges, especially in the context of elections. With the potential to create highly realistic and convincing fake videos and audio, AI-generated misinformation has the power to sway public opinion and undermine the democratic process. This trend highlights the urgent need for robust measures to detect and mitigate misinformation before it spreads like wildfire.

One of the key areas where AI-generated misinformation is particularly concerning is in the realm of political propaganda. With the ability to create fake news stories, videos, and social media posts that appear to come from legitimate sources, AI-generated disinformation can be used to manipulate public opinion and influence election outcomes. It is crucial for professionals in this field to stay vigilant and develop effective strategies to combat this growing threat.

In addition to political propaganda, AI-generated fake news is also a major concern in other industries such as healthcare, finance, entertainment, education, cybersecurity, climate change, and international relations. In healthcare, for example, AI-generated disinformation can lead to dangerous misinformation about treatments, vaccines, and public health policies. In finance, it can impact stock prices and investor confidence. In entertainment, it can create fake celebrity gossip or reviews. In education, it can mislead students with false information. In cybersecurity, it can be used to spread malware or launch phishing attacks. In climate change, it can sow doubt about the scientific consensus on global warming. In international relations, it can be used to incite conflict or destabilize governments.

To effectively combat AI-generated misinformation in all these areas, professionals must work together to develop robust detection and mitigation strategies. This may involve using advanced AI algorithms to analyze and identify fake content, working with social media platforms to remove harmful material, educating the public about the dangers of misinformation, and collaborating with policymakers to create regulations that hold perpetrators accountable. By taking proactive measures to address this growing threat, professionals can help protect the integrity of information and safeguard society from the harmful effects of AI-generated disinformation.

Chapter 2: AI-generated Political Propaganda

Impact on elections

The impact of AI-generated misinformation on elections cannot be understated. With the rise of deepfakes and AI-generated content, political propaganda has taken on a new level of sophistication and reach. This has serious implications for the integrity of democratic processes, as false information can sway public opinion and influence election outcomes. It is essential for professionals in the field of cybersecurity, politics, and media to be aware of these challenges and take proactive measures to combat them.

One of the key issues surrounding AI-generated misinformation in elections is the difficulty in detecting it. Unlike traditional forms of misinformation, AI-generated content can be incredibly realistic and difficult to distinguish from genuine information. This makes it all the more dangerous, as unsuspecting voters may be swayed by false narratives without even realizing it. Professionals must rely on advanced technologies and techniques to identify and counteract this type of disinformation.

AI-generated fake news is another major concern in the context of elections. False stories spread rapidly on social media platforms, reaching millions of users in a matter of hours. This can have a significant impact on public opinion and voter behavior, potentially leading to the election of unqualified or unsuitable candidates. It is crucial for professionals to work together to monitor and combat the spread of fake news during election periods, ensuring that voters have access to accurate and reliable information.

Social media manipulation is yet another challenge posed by AI-generated misinformation in elections. Bots and fake accounts can be used to amplify certain messages and suppress others, creating a distorted view of public sentiment. This can be particularly damaging in the lead-up to an election, as it can skew the narrative and influence voter behavior. Professionals must be vigilant in monitoring social media activity and taking action against accounts that engage in manipulative behavior.

In conclusion, the impact of AI-generated misinformation on elections is a serious and growing concern. Professionals must be proactive in detecting and mitigating this type of disinformation, using advanced technologies and strategies to ensure the integrity of democratic processes. By working together to combat fake news, political propaganda, and social media manipulation, we can protect the sanctity of elections and uphold the principles of democracy.

Strategies for detecting AI-generated political propaganda

In the age of advanced technology, detecting AI-generated political propaganda has become a crucial task for professionals in various industries. As AI-generated content, including deepfakes, continues to evolve, the spread of misinformation and propaganda has become more prevalent, especially in the context of elections. To combat this growing threat, professionals must implement robust strategies to detect and mitigate AI-generated political propaganda effectively.

One key strategy for detecting AI-generated political propaganda is the use of advanced machine learning algorithms. By leveraging AI technology, professionals can analyze vast amounts of data to identify patterns and anomalies that may indicate the presence of propaganda. These algorithms can be trained to recognize specific characteristics of AI-generated content, such as unnatural language patterns or inconsistencies in audio or video recordings, helping professionals to flag potential instances of misinformation.

Another effective strategy for detecting AI-generated political propaganda is the use of network analysis tools. By monitoring the flow of information across social media platforms and online channels, professionals can track the spread of propaganda and identify the sources of false information. Network analysis tools can also help professionals to identify coordinated campaigns aimed at manipulating public opinion, allowing them to take proactive measures to counteract these efforts.

Additionally, professionals can enhance their detection capabilities by collaborating with experts in the field of AI ethics and misinformation. By working with researchers, academics, and other professionals who specialize in detecting and mitigating AI-generated misinformation, professionals can stay ahead of the latest developments in the field and develop new strategies for combating propaganda. This collaborative approach can help professionals to leverage the collective expertise of the broader community and enhance their ability to detect and mitigate AI-generated political propaganda effectively.

Ultimately, the fight against AI-generated political propaganda requires a multi-faceted approach that combines advanced technology, strategic analysis, and collaboration among professionals from various disciplines. By implementing robust detection strategies, professionals can help to safeguard the integrity of elections and protect the public from the harmful effects of misinformation. With continued vigilance and innovation, professionals can stay one step ahead of those seeking to manipulate public opinion and ensure a more informed and democratic society.

Chapter 3: AI-generated Fake News

Spread of fake news through AI

The spread of fake news through AI has become a growing concern in today's digital age. With the rise of AI-generated content, including deepfakes, the dissemination of misinformation has reached unprecedented levels. This trend is particularly alarming in the context of elections, where AI-generated political propaganda can sway public opinion and undermine the democratic process. As professionals in the field of AI, it is imperative that we take proactive measures to detect and mitigate the spread of fake news through AI.

One of the key challenges in combating AI-generated misinformation is the ability of AI algorithms to create highly convincing content that is difficult to distinguish from real information. This has led to the proliferation of AI-generated fake news across various platforms, including social media. As professionals, it is our responsibility to develop robust measures to identify and debunk fake news generated by AI, in order to protect the integrity of our information ecosystem.

AI-generated disinformation is not limited to political propaganda. It also extends to other sectors such as healthcare, finance, entertainment, education, cybersecurity, climate change, and international relations. In healthcare, for example, AI-generated misinformation can spread false medical advice or promote dangerous treatments. In finance, it can manipulate markets and deceive investors. In entertainment, it can create fake celebrity news or reviews. In education, it can distort historical facts or spread false information. In cybersecurity, it can be used to launch sophisticated phishing attacks or spread malware. In climate change, it can distort scientific findings or downplay the severity of the crisis. In international relations, it can manipulate public opinion or sow discord between nations.

As professionals, we must work together to develop effective strategies for detecting and mitigating AI-generated misinformation across all sectors. This may involve leveraging AI technologies to identify fake news, collaborating with experts in various fields to verify information, and educating the public on how to critically evaluate the information they encounter online. By taking a proactive approach to combating AI-generated disinformation, we can help safeguard the integrity of our information ecosystem and protect society from the harmful effects of fake news.

Tools for identifying AI-generated fake news

In the digital age, the rise of AI-generated content, including deepfakes, has posed new challenges, particularly in the context of elections. With the increasing prevalence of AI-generated misinformation, there is a pressing need for professionals to have robust tools at their disposal to accurately identify and mitigate these issues. This subchapter will delve into the various tools available for detecting AI-generated fake news, providing practical guidance for professionals in navigating this complex landscape.

One key tool for identifying AI-generated fake news is the use of natural language processing (NLP) techniques. NLP can help professionals analyze text data and detect patterns that may indicate the presence of AI-generated content. By leveraging NLP tools, professionals can better understand the language used in fake news articles and identify discrepancies that suggest the involvement of AI algorithms in their creation.

Another valuable tool for professionals is the use of image analysis algorithms to detect deepfakes. Deepfakes are AI-generated videos or images that manipulate visual content to deceive viewers. By utilizing image analysis algorithms, professionals can scrutinize the visual elements of content and identify subtle inconsistencies that may indicate the presence of AI manipulation. This tool can be particularly useful in the context of political propaganda, where deepfakes can be used to spread false information and sway public opinion.

Social media monitoring tools are also essential for identifying AI-generated fake news. These tools allow professionals to track the spread of misinformation on popular social media platforms and identify patterns that may indicate the involvement of AI algorithms. By monitoring social media activity, professionals can quickly identify and respond to instances of AI-generated disinformation, helping to prevent its spread and mitigate its impact on public discourse.

In addition to these technical tools, professionals can also benefit from collaborating with interdisciplinary teams that include experts in AI, data science, and psychology. By combining expertise from different fields, professionals can gain a more comprehensive understanding of AI-generated fake news and develop effective strategies for detecting and mitigating its impact. This holistic approach can help professionals stay ahead of the curve in combating the spread of AI-generated misinformation across various sectors, from politics to healthcare to finance.

Overall, the tools for identifying AI-generated fake news are constantly evolving as the landscape of AI-generated content continues to change. By staying informed about the latest developments in technology and collaborating with experts in relevant fields, professionals can better equip themselves to detect and mitigate the spread of AI-generated misinformation in today's digital age.

Chapter 4: AI-generated Social Media Manipulation

Techniques used for social media manipulation

In the digital age, social media manipulation has become a prevalent issue, with AI-generated content making it even more challenging to detect and combat. In the context of elections, AI-generated disinformation can sway public opinion and undermine the democratic process. To address this growing concern, professionals must be equipped with the necessary tools and techniques to identify and mitigate the spread of misinformation on social media platforms.

One technique used for social media manipulation is the creation of AI-generated political propaganda. By using advanced algorithms, malicious actors can create persuasive content that is designed to deceive and influence voters. Professionals must be vigilant in monitoring social media platforms for suspicious activity and take proactive measures to counteract these efforts.

Another common tactic used for social media manipulation is the dissemination of AI-generated fake news. This type of disinformation is designed to mimic legitimate news sources and can spread rapidly on social media platforms. Professionals must be able to distinguish between fact and fiction and work to debunk false information before it gains traction among the public.

In addition to political propaganda and fake news, AI-generated social media manipulation can also be used to spread disinformation in other sectors such as healthcare, finance, entertainment, education, cybersecurity, climate change, and international relations. Professionals must be aware of the various ways in which AI-generated content can be used to manipulate public opinion and take proactive measures to combat these efforts.

Overall, detecting and mitigating AI-generated misinformation requires a multi-faceted approach that involves monitoring social media platforms, analyzing trends, and collaborating with other professionals in the field. By staying informed and implementing robust measures to combat social media manipulation, professionals can help safeguard the integrity of online information and protect the public from falling victim to AI-generated disinformation.

Countermeasures for combating AI-generated social media manipulation

In the digital age, social media has become a powerful tool for spreading information and influencing public opinion. However, with the rise of AI-generated content, including deepfakes, the landscape of social media manipulation has become increasingly complex. This trend poses new challenges, especially in the context of elections, where misinformation can have serious consequences for democracy. As such, professionals must be equipped with robust measures to combat AI-generated social media manipulation.

One key countermeasure for combating AI-generated social media manipulation is the use of AI-powered detection tools. These tools can analyze patterns in online behavior and content to identify suspicious activity, such as the spread of fake news or propaganda. By leveraging AI technology, professionals can stay one step ahead of those who seek to manipulate social media for their own gain.

Another important countermeasure is the implementation of fact-checking mechanisms. Professionals can use AI algorithms to verify the accuracy of information circulating on social media platforms. By cross-referencing data with reliable sources and flagging potentially false content, professionals can help prevent the spread of misinformation and disinformation.

Additionally, professionals can work to improve digital literacy among the public to help them discern fact from fiction online. By educating users about the tactics used by AI-generated content creators, professionals can empower individuals to critically evaluate the information they encounter on social media. This can help inoculate the public against the effects of social media manipulation.

Furthermore, collaboration between tech companies, policymakers, and researchers is essential for developing comprehensive strategies to combat AI-generated social media manipulation. By sharing resources, expertise, and data, these stakeholders can work together to create a more secure online environment. By working together, professionals can stay ahead of the curve in the fight against AI-generated misinformation and disinformation on social media platforms.

Chapter 5: AI-generated Disinformation in Healthcare

Threats posed by AI-generated disinformation in healthcare

AI-generated disinformation in healthcare is a growing concern that professionals in the industry must address. The advancement of artificial intelligence technology has enabled the creation of highly convincing fake content that can spread misinformation about healthcare practices, treatments, and medical research. This poses a serious threat to public health as individuals may make decisions based on false information, leading to harmful consequences for themselves and others.

One of the primary challenges posed by AI-generated disinformation in healthcare is the difficulty in detecting it. Unlike traditional forms of misinformation, AI-generated content can be incredibly realistic and difficult to distinguish from legitimate sources. This makes it crucial for professionals to develop sophisticated tools and strategies for identifying and combating fake healthcare information before it spreads widely and causes harm.

Another significant concern is the potential for AI-generated disinformation to manipulate public perceptions of healthcare providers, treatments, and practices. By spreading false information, malicious actors can undermine trust in legitimate healthcare institutions and professionals, leading to a breakdown in the doctor-patient relationship and potentially impacting public health outcomes. Professionals must be vigilant in monitoring online platforms for signs of AI-generated disinformation and take swift action to address any misleading content that may be circulating.

Furthermore, the spread of AI-generated disinformation in healthcare can have far-reaching consequences for vulnerable populations. For example, false information about certain medical treatments or procedures could prevent individuals from seeking necessary care, leading to worsened health outcomes or even death. Professionals must work together to develop strategies for reaching these populations with accurate information and countering the spread of fake content that may put their health at risk.

In conclusion, the rise of AI-generated disinformation in healthcare presents a significant challenge for professionals in the industry. By developing robust detection and mitigation strategies, healthcare professionals can help protect public health and ensure that individuals have access to accurate information about their health and well-being. It is essential for professionals to stay informed about the latest developments in AI technology and work together to combat the spread of fake healthcare information online.

Approaches for addressing misinformation in the healthcare sector

In the healthcare sector, misinformation can have serious consequences, potentially leading to incorrect diagnoses, delayed treatment, or even harm to patients. As AI technology continues to advance, the spread of misinformation in healthcare is becoming increasingly prevalent. It is crucial for professionals in the healthcare industry to be aware of the various approaches for addressing and combating this issue.

One approach for addressing misinformation in the healthcare sector is through the use of AI-powered tools and technologies. These tools can help to identify and flag incorrect or misleading information, allowing healthcare professionals to quickly assess and correct any misinformation that may be circulating. By leveraging AI technology in this way, healthcare organizations can more effectively combat the spread of false information and ensure that patients receive accurate and reliable healthcare advice.

Another approach is through the implementation of robust fact-checking processes. By verifying the accuracy of information before it is shared or disseminated, healthcare professionals can help to prevent the spread of misinformation within their organizations. Fact-checking tools and techniques can be used to evaluate the credibility of sources, cross-reference information with reputable sources, and identify any inconsistencies or inaccuracies in the information being presented.

Collaboration with other healthcare professionals and organizations is also key in addressing misinformation in the healthcare sector. By working together to share information, resources, and best practices, healthcare professionals can more effectively identify and address instances of misinformation. This collaborative approach can help to strengthen the healthcare industry's ability to combat misinformation and ensure that patients receive accurate and reliable information.

Education and training are also important tools for addressing misinformation in the healthcare sector. By providing healthcare professionals with the knowledge and skills they need to identify and address misinformation, organizations can help to prevent the spread of false information and promote the dissemination of accurate and reliable healthcare advice. Training programs can help professionals to recognize common types of misinformation, understand the potential impact of false information on patient care, and develop strategies for effectively addressing and correcting misinformation when it arises.

Overall, a multi-faceted approach is needed to effectively address misinformation in the healthcare sector. By leveraging AI-powered tools, implementing robust fact-checking processes, collaborating with other healthcare professionals and organizations, and providing education and training to healthcare professionals, organizations can work together to combat the spread of false information and ensure that patients receive accurate and reliable healthcare advice. By taking proactive measures to address misinformation, professionals in the healthcare sector can help to protect the integrity of the industry and the well-being of their patients.

Chapter 6: AI-generated Disinformation in Finance

Impact of AI-generated disinformation on financial markets

The impact of AI-generated disinformation on financial markets cannot be underestimated. With the rise of AI technology, the dissemination of false information has become more sophisticated and harder to detect. This has serious implications for investors, traders, and financial institutions, as misinformation can distort market trends, manipulate stock prices, and cause significant financial losses.

One of the key challenges posed by AI-generated disinformation in financial markets is the speed at which false information can spread. With the help of AI algorithms, malicious actors can create and distribute fake news or rumors that can quickly influence market sentiment and trigger panic selling or buying. This can lead to market volatility and instability, making it difficult for investors to make informed decisions.

Moreover, AI-generated disinformation can also be used to manipulate stock prices for personal gain. By spreading false information about a company's financial performance or future prospects, malicious actors can artificially inflate or deflate stock prices, leading to significant financial gains or losses. This poses a serious threat to the integrity and transparency of financial markets, as well as the trust of investors in the market.

Detecting and mitigating AI-generated disinformation in financial markets requires a multi-faceted approach. Financial institutions and regulatory bodies need to invest in advanced AI technologies and algorithms to detect and filter out fake news and rumors in real-time. They also need to collaborate with cybersecurity experts and law enforcement agencies to identify and prosecute malicious actors who engage in market manipulation through disinformation.

Overall, the impact of AI-generated disinformation on financial markets is a growing concern that requires immediate attention and action. By understanding the risks and challenges posed by AI technology, financial professionals can better protect themselves and their investments from the damaging effects of fake news and misinformation.

Steps for mitigating financial fraud through AI

Financial fraud is a growing concern in today's digital age, with criminals constantly finding new ways to exploit vulnerabilities in systems and processes. One potential solution to combat this issue is the use of artificial intelligence (AI) technology. By leveraging AI tools, organizations can proactively detect and mitigate financial fraud before it causes significant harm.

The first step in mitigating financial fraud through AI is to implement robust data analytics systems that can identify patterns and anomalies in financial transactions. AI algorithms can analyze vast amounts of data in real-time, flagging any suspicious activities that may indicate fraudulent behavior. By continuously monitoring transactions, organizations can stay one step ahead of fraudsters and prevent potential losses.

Another crucial step in combating financial fraud is the use of AI-powered predictive modeling. By analyzing historical data and trends, AI algorithms can predict future fraudulent activities and help organizations take preemptive measures to prevent them. This proactive approach can significantly reduce the risk of financial fraud and save organizations time and resources in the long run.

Furthermore, organizations should consider implementing AI-powered fraud detection tools that can automatically detect and block fraudulent transactions in real-time. These tools can analyze various data points, such as transaction amounts, frequencies, and locations, to identify fraudulent activities and prevent them before they escalate. By automating the fraud detection process, organizations can streamline their operations and improve their overall security posture.

In conclusion, mitigating financial fraud through AI requires a multi-faceted approach that combines data analytics, predictive modeling, and automated fraud detection tools. By leveraging AI technology, organizations can proactively detect and prevent fraudulent activities, ultimately safeguarding their assets and reputation. As financial fraud continues to evolve, it is essential for professionals to stay informed about the latest AI-driven solutions and implement them effectively to protect their organizations from potential threats.

Chapter 7: AI-generated Disinformation in Entertainment

Influence of AI-generated content on the entertainment industry

In recent years, the entertainment industry has seen a significant impact from the rise of AI-generated content. From deepfake videos to AI-generated music and scripts, artificial intelligence is revolutionizing the way content is created and consumed. This shift has presented both opportunities and challenges for professionals in the entertainment sector, as they navigate the complexities of this new technology.

One of the key areas where AI-generated content is making an impact is in the creation of digital influencers. These virtual personalities, often created using AI algorithms, have the potential to reach millions of followers and influence consumer behavior. This trend has raised concerns about the authenticity of these influencers and the potential for AI-generated content to manipulate audiences for commercial gain.

Another area where AI-generated content is shaping the entertainment industry is in the production of films and television shows. AI algorithms are now being used to analyze audience preferences and predict box office success, leading to the creation of more targeted and profitable content. However, this reliance on data-driven decision-making has also raised questions about the creativity and originality of AI-generated entertainment.

Furthermore, the rise of AI-generated content has blurred the lines between reality and fiction in the entertainment industry. Deepfake technology, which uses AI algorithms to manipulate images and videos, has made it increasingly difficult to discern what is real and what is fake. This has led to concerns about the potential for AI-generated content to spread misinformation and deceive audiences.

Overall, the influence of AI-generated content on the entertainment industry is undeniable. As professionals in this sector, it is essential to stay informed about the latest developments in AI technology and take proactive measures to detect and mitigate the spread of misinformation. By understanding the opportunities and challenges presented by AI-generated content, professionals can harness the power of this technology while also safeguarding the integrity of the entertainment industry.

Strategies for identifying and combating misinformation in entertainment

In the realm of entertainment, misinformation can spread rapidly and have significant consequences. From fake celebrity news to manipulated videos, the entertainment industry is not immune to the threat of AI-generated disinformation. Professionals in this field must be vigilant and proactive in identifying and combating misinformation to maintain the integrity of their work and protect their audience.

One key strategy for identifying misinformation in entertainment is to stay informed and up-to-date on the latest trends and technologies used to create fake content. By understanding how AI can be used to manipulate images, videos, and audio, professionals can better recognize when something may be inaccurate or misleading. Additionally, collaborating with experts in AI and digital forensics can provide valuable insights and tools for detecting deepfakes and other forms of disinformation.

Another effective strategy is to establish clear guidelines and standards for verifying the authenticity of content before sharing it with the public. This may involve implementing fact-checking processes, conducting thorough research, and consulting multiple sources to confirm the accuracy of information. By setting high standards for the content they produce and promote, professionals can help prevent the spread of misinformation in the entertainment industry.

Furthermore, professionals can leverage technology and AI tools to aid in the detection and mitigation of misinformation. Machine learning algorithms can be used to analyze large datasets and identify patterns that may indicate the presence of fake content. Additionally, digital watermarking and blockchain technology can help track the origin and authenticity of media files, making it easier to verify their legitimacy.

Lastly, fostering a culture of transparency and accountability within the entertainment industry can help combat misinformation. By being open and honest about the risks of AI-generated disinformation and the steps being taken to address them, professionals can build trust with their audience and demonstrate a commitment to ethical practices. By working together to address this growing threat, professionals in entertainment can protect the integrity of their work and ensure that accurate information prevails in a world increasingly saturated with fake content.

Chapter 8: AI-generated Disinformation in Education

Role of AI-generated content in education

In the field of education, the role of AI-generated content is becoming increasingly significant. As technology continues to advance, the use of AI in creating educational materials has opened up new possibilities for both teachers and students. AI-generated content can help educators personalize learning experiences, provide real-time feedback, and offer interactive resources that cater to individual student needs.

One of the key benefits of AI-generated content in education is its ability to adapt to the unique learning styles and preferences of each student. By analyzing data on student performance and behavior, AI algorithms can create customized learning materials that target areas where students may need extra help or challenge them with more advanced concepts. This personalized approach can lead to better academic outcomes and increased engagement in the learning process.

Additionally, AI-generated content can help teachers save time by automating tasks such as grading assignments, creating lesson plans, and generating practice exercises. This allows educators to focus more on providing one-on-one support to students and fostering a collaborative learning environment. By offloading routine tasks to AI systems, teachers can free up valuable time to focus on more strategic aspects of their teaching practice.

Furthermore, AI-generated content can enhance the accessibility of education by providing resources in multiple formats, such as audio, video, and interactive simulations. This can benefit students with diverse learning needs, including those with disabilities or language barriers. By leveraging AI technology, educators can create inclusive learning environments that cater to the needs of all learners, regardless of their background or abilities.

Overall, the use of AI-generated content in education holds great promise for improving learning outcomes, increasing efficiency, and promoting inclusivity in the classroom. However, it is crucial for educators to be aware of the potential risks and challenges associated with AI-generated materials, such as bias in algorithms, privacy concerns, and the need for human oversight. By staying informed and adopting best practices for using AI in education, professionals can harness the power of technology to enhance the learning experience for all students.

Measures for preventing the spread of misinformation in educational settings

In educational settings, the spread of misinformation can have serious consequences on students' learning and understanding of various subjects. To prevent the dissemination of false information, it is essential for educators to implement measures that promote critical thinking skills and fact-checking abilities among students. By teaching students how to evaluate the credibility of sources and verify information before sharing it, educators can empower them to be more discerning consumers of information.

One effective measure for preventing the spread of misinformation in educational settings is to incorporate media literacy education into the curriculum. By teaching students how to critically analyze and interpret media messages, educators can help them develop the skills needed to identify misinformation and disinformation. Media literacy education can also help students understand the motivations behind the creation of misleading content and how to spot red flags that indicate potential falsehoods.

Another important measure for preventing the spread of misinformation in educational settings is to promote digital literacy among students. This includes teaching students how to navigate the digital landscape responsibly, including how to spot fake news, identify bots and trolls, and protect their personal information online. By equipping students with the knowledge and skills needed to navigate the digital world safely, educators can help reduce the likelihood of them falling victim to misinformation.

Educators can also play a key role in preventing the spread of misinformation by fostering an environment of open dialogue and critical thinking in the classroom. By encouraging students to question sources, challenge assumptions, and engage in respectful debate, educators can help create a culture of skepticism and inquiry that is essential for combating misinformation. By promoting a healthy skepticism towards information and encouraging students to seek out multiple perspectives on a given topic, educators can help build resilience against the spread of misinformation.

Overall, preventing the spread of misinformation in educational settings requires a multi-faceted approach that includes promoting media literacy, digital literacy, critical thinking, and open dialogue. By equipping students with the knowledge and skills needed to critically evaluate information and engage in responsible online behavior, educators can help mitigate the impact of misinformation on their learning and development. It is essential for educators to stay informed about the latest trends in AI-generated misinformation and adapt their strategies accordingly to ensure that students are prepared to navigate the complex digital landscape with confidence and discernment.

Chapter 9: AI-generated Disinformation in Cybersecurity

Threats of AI-generated disinformation in cybersecurity

In today's digital age, the rise of AI-generated disinformation poses a significant threat to cybersecurity. With the advancement of technology, malicious actors are now able to create highly realistic fake content, such as deepfakes, that can deceive even the most discerning eye. This trend is particularly concerning in the context of elections, where misinformation can sway public opinion and undermine the democratic process. As such, professionals in the cybersecurity field must be vigilant in detecting and mitigating AI-generated disinformation to protect critical systems and data.

One of the key challenges posed by AI-generated disinformation is the difficulty in distinguishing between genuine and fake content. With AI algorithms becoming increasingly sophisticated, it is becoming harder to identify manipulated or fabricated information. This makes it easier for malicious actors to spread false narratives and manipulate public perception. Professionals in cybersecurity must therefore develop robust measures to detect AI-generated disinformation and prevent its harmful effects.

AI-generated political propaganda is another major concern in the realm of cybersecurity. Political campaigns are increasingly relying on AI technology to target voters with personalized messaging, making it easier for them to spread misinformation and manipulate public opinion. This poses a serious threat to the integrity of elections and democratic processes. Detecting and mitigating AI-generated political propaganda requires a multi-faceted approach that includes monitoring social media platforms, analyzing data patterns, and collaborating with policymakers to enforce regulations.

AI-generated fake news is also a growing problem in cybersecurity. With the proliferation of social media platforms and online news outlets, fake news can spread rapidly and reach a wide audience. Malicious actors can use AI algorithms to create and disseminate false information, causing confusion and distrust among the public. Professionals in cybersecurity must work to develop tools and techniques to identify and combat AI-generated fake news, in order to protect the integrity of information and prevent harm to individuals and organizations.

In conclusion, the threats of AI-generated disinformation in cybersecurity are real and pressing. As technology continues to advance, it is crucial for professionals in the field to stay ahead of the curve and develop effective strategies to detect and mitigate misinformation. By understanding the challenges posed by AI-generated disinformation, professionals can work towards creating a safer and more secure digital environment for all.

Best practices for protecting against AI-driven cyber attacks

As AI-driven cyber attacks become increasingly prevalent, it is crucial for professionals to implement best practices to protect against them. One of the most important steps is to regularly update security protocols and software to defend against evolving threats. This includes implementing strong encryption methods, multi-factor authentication, and regular security audits to identify and patch vulnerabilities before they can be exploited by malicious actors.

Another key practice is to educate employees on the dangers of AI-driven cyber attacks and how to recognize potential threats. Training programs should focus on teaching staff how to identify phishing emails, suspicious links, and other common tactics used by hackers to gain access to sensitive information. By raising awareness and fostering a culture of cybersecurity within the organization, professionals can help mitigate the risks of AI-driven cyber attacks.

In addition to employee training, professionals should also consider investing in AI-powered cybersecurity tools to help detect and respond to threats in real-time. These tools can analyze vast amounts of data to identify patterns and anomalies that may indicate a cyber attack is underway. By leveraging AI technology to enhance their security measures, professionals can stay one step ahead of hackers and protect their sensitive data more effectively.

Furthermore, professionals should establish strict access controls and permissions to limit the exposure of sensitive information to potential threats. By restricting access to only those who need it, organizations can reduce the risk of insider threats and unauthorized access to critical systems. Regularly reviewing and updating access controls can help prevent unauthorized access and minimize the impact of AI-driven cyber attacks.

Overall, by implementing these best practices for protecting against AI-driven cyber attacks, professionals can strengthen their cybersecurity posture and better defend against the growing threats posed by AI-generated misinformation. By staying informed, educating employees, leveraging AI technology, and establishing strict access controls, professionals can proactively defend their organizations against cyber threats and safeguard their data from malicious actors.

Chapter 10: AI-generated Disinformation in Climate Change

Impact of AI-generated misinformation on climate change discourse

The impact of AI-generated misinformation on the discourse surrounding climate change is significant and worrisome. As artificial intelligence continues to advance, so too do the capabilities of those seeking to spread false information for various purposes. With the rise of deepfake technology, it has become increasingly difficult to discern what is true and what is fabricated in the realm of climate change discussions.

One of the most concerning aspects of AI-generated misinformation on climate change is its potential to sway public opinion and policy decisions. By disseminating false information through AI-powered tools, malicious actors can manipulate the public's perception of the severity of climate change and the urgency of taking action. This can have far-reaching consequences for how governments and organizations address the issue, potentially leading to delays in implementing crucial measures to mitigate the effects of climate change.

Furthermore, the spread of AI-generated misinformation on climate change can also erode trust in legitimate sources of information. As more and more false narratives are perpetuated through AI-powered platforms, it becomes increasingly challenging for individuals to discern fact from fiction. This can lead to confusion and apathy among the public, hindering efforts to raise awareness and mobilize action on climate change.

In order to combat the impact of AI-generated misinformation on climate change discourse, professionals must be proactive in developing robust detection and mitigation strategies. This includes investing in AI-powered tools that can help identify and flag false information, as well as educating the public on how to critically evaluate the sources of information they encounter. By staying vigilant and informed, professionals can help combat the spread of AI-generated misinformation and ensure that accurate information prevails in the discourse on climate change.

Ultimately, the impact of AI-generated misinformation on climate change discourse underscores the importance of remaining vigilant and proactive in the face of evolving technological threats. By recognizing the potential risks posed by AI-powered tools in spreading false information, professionals can take steps to safeguard the integrity of climate change discussions and ensure that accurate information prevails. Only through a concerted effort to combat misinformation can we hope to address the urgent challenges posed by climate change and work towards a sustainable future for all.

Initiatives for promoting accurate information on climate issues

Initiatives for promoting accurate information on climate issues are crucial in combating the spread of AI-generated disinformation in this area. As climate change becomes an increasingly urgent global concern, it is essential that professionals take proactive steps to ensure that accurate information is disseminated to the public. One key initiative is the development of AI-powered tools that can help detect and flag misleading or false information related to climate change. These tools can analyze large amounts of data from various sources to identify patterns of misinformation and alert users to potential inaccuracies.

Another important initiative is the establishment of partnerships between tech companies, government agencies, and non-profit organizations to collaborate on strategies for combating AI-generated disinformation on climate issues. By working together, these stakeholders can share resources, expertise, and best practices to develop more effective solutions for addressing this growing problem. Additionally, these partnerships can help raise awareness among the public about the dangers of misinformation and the importance of seeking out reliable sources of information on climate change.

Furthermore, professionals can play a key role in promoting media literacy and critical thinking skills among the public to help them discern between accurate and misleading information on climate issues. By providing education and training on how to evaluate sources, fact-check information, and identify red flags of misinformation, professionals can empower individuals to make informed decisions and resist the influence of AI-generated disinformation. This can help build a more resilient society that is better equipped to navigate the complex landscape of digital information.

In addition, professionals can support efforts to enhance transparency and accountability in the digital ecosystem to prevent the spread of AI-generated disinformation on climate change. This includes advocating for policies that promote greater transparency in online platforms, such as requiring disclosure of the sources of information and the use of algorithms to prioritize content. By promoting greater accountability among tech companies and social media platforms, professionals can help create a more trustworthy online environment where accurate information on climate issues can thrive.

Overall, initiatives for promoting accurate information on climate issues are essential for combating the spread of AI-generated disinformation in this critical area. By leveraging AI-powered tools, forming partnerships, promoting media literacy, and advocating for transparency and accountability, professionals can help safeguard the public discourse on climate change and ensure that accurate information prevails over misinformation. By working together, we can build a more informed and resilient society that is better equipped to address the challenges of climate change in the digital age.

Chapter 11: AI-generated Disinformation in International Relations

Use of AI in spreading disinformation in global politics

The use of artificial intelligence (AI) in spreading disinformation in global politics has become a growing concern in recent years. The rise of AI-generated content, including deepfakes, has made it easier than ever for malicious actors to create and spread false information on a massive scale. This trend is particularly troubling in the context of elections, where misinformation can have a significant impact on the outcome of political campaigns.

AI-generated political propaganda is a particularly insidious form of disinformation, as it can be tailored to target specific groups of voters with highly persuasive messaging. This type of propaganda can be used to sow division, spread false information about political candidates, and undermine the democratic process. Detecting and mitigating AI-generated political propaganda is essential to ensuring the integrity of elections and protecting the public from manipulation.

AI-generated fake news is another major concern in global politics, as it can be used to spread false information about political events, policies, and individuals. This type of disinformation can have far-reaching consequences, influencing public opinion, shaping political discourse, and even inciting violence. Detecting and combating AI-generated fake news requires a multi-faceted approach that involves both technological solutions and human intervention.

AI-generated social media manipulation is also a significant issue in global politics, as it can be used to amplify false information, manipulate public opinion, and influence political outcomes. Malicious actors can use AI algorithms to create and spread fake accounts, bots, and automated messages that are designed to deceive and manipulate social media users. Detecting and mitigating AI-generated social media manipulation requires close collaboration between tech companies, governments, and civil society organizations.

In conclusion, the use of AI in spreading disinformation in global politics presents a serious threat to the integrity of democratic processes and the stability of societies around the world. Detecting and mitigating AI-generated misinformation requires a coordinated and multi-disciplinary approach that combines technological solutions, policy interventions, and public awareness campaigns. By working together to address this growing threat, we can protect the public from manipulation and ensure that our democracies remain strong and resilient in the face of new challenges.

Diplomatic efforts to combat AI-generated misinformation on the international stage

In the ever-evolving landscape of AI-generated misinformation, diplomatic efforts are crucial in combating the spread of false information on the international stage. As AI technologies continue to advance, the potential for malicious actors to use these tools to manipulate public opinion and sow discord has become a growing concern. This subchapter explores the role of diplomacy in addressing the challenges posed by AI-generated misinformation, particularly in the context of international relations.

One key aspect of diplomatic efforts to combat AI-generated misinformation is the need for collaboration and information sharing among countries. Given the borderless nature of the internet, no single nation can tackle this issue alone. By working together, countries can share best practices, intelligence, and resources to more effectively identify and counteract malicious AI-generated content. This collaborative approach is essential in building a united front against the spread of misinformation on a global scale.

Another important aspect of diplomatic efforts is the need for international agreements and regulations to govern the use of AI technologies in the dissemination of information. As AI-generated content becomes increasingly sophisticated, it is crucial to establish clear guidelines to prevent its misuse for malicious purposes. By developing international standards and protocols, countries can create a framework for addressing the challenges posed by AI-generated misinformation in a coordinated and consistent manner.

Furthermore, diplomatic efforts can play a crucial role in promoting transparency and accountability among tech companies and social media platforms. By engaging with these stakeholders on an international level, governments can encourage greater responsibility in the development and deployment of AI technologies. This can help to prevent the spread of AI-generated misinformation and ensure that these platforms are used ethically and responsibly.

In conclusion, diplomatic efforts are essential in the fight against AI-generated misinformation on the international stage. By fostering collaboration, establishing regulations, and promoting transparency, countries can work together to address the challenges posed by malicious AI-generated content. Through these diplomatic initiatives, professionals can help to create a safer and more secure online environment for all users.

Chapter 12: Conclusion and Future Outlook

Summary of key points

Summary of key points:

1. The rise of AI-generated content, including deepfakes, is posing new challenges in various sectors such as politics, healthcare, finance, entertainment, education, cybersecurity, climate change, and international relations. This trend highlights the need for robust measures to detect and mitigate misinformation spread through AI-generated means.

2. AI-generated political propaganda is a growing concern, as it has the potential to manipulate public opinion and influence election outcomes. Professionals need to be vigilant in detecting and combating AI-generated disinformation in the political sphere to ensure fair and transparent democratic processes.

3. AI-generated fake news is a pervasive issue that can spread rapidly on social media platforms, leading to widespread confusion and mistrust. Professionals must be equipped with the tools and knowledge to identify and debunk false information generated by AI algorithms.

4. AI-generated social media manipulation is a tactic used by malicious actors to sway public opinion, incite division, and spread misinformation. Professionals working in social media and digital marketing must be proactive in detecting and countering AI-generated disinformation campaigns.

5. The spread of AI-generated disinformation in sectors such as healthcare, finance, entertainment, education, cybersecurity, climate change, and international relations can have far-reaching consequences. Professionals in these fields must collaborate and implement strategies to combat the spread of false information generated by AI technologies. By staying informed, vigilant, and proactive, professionals can help mitigate the harmful effects of AI-generated misinformation on society.

Recommendations for professionals in combating AI-generated misinformation

In combating AI-generated misinformation, professionals must first prioritize staying abreast of the latest developments and trends in AI technology. This includes understanding how AI is being used to generate misinformation across various sectors such as politics, healthcare, finance, entertainment, education, cybersecurity, climate change, and international relations. By keeping up-to-date with the evolving landscape of AI-generated disinformation, professionals can better anticipate and respond to emerging threats.

Secondly, professionals should work towards enhancing their technical skills in order to effectively detect and mitigate AI-generated misinformation. This may involve gaining expertise in AI algorithms, machine learning, natural language processing, and other relevant technologies. By developing a strong technical foundation, professionals will be better equipped to identify patterns and anomalies in AI-generated content, enabling them to take proactive measures to combat misinformation.

Collaboration and information sharing are also key recommendations for professionals in the fight against AI-generated misinformation. By working together with other experts in the field, professionals can leverage collective knowledge and resources to develop more effective strategies for detecting and mitigating misinformation. Additionally, sharing best practices and lessons learned can help to build a stronger defense against AI-generated disinformation across different sectors.

Furthermore, professionals should prioritize transparency and accountability in their efforts to combat AI-generated misinformation. This includes being open about the methods and tools used to detect and mitigate misinformation, as well as being accountable for the outcomes of their actions. By operating with transparency and accountability, professionals can build trust with stakeholders and demonstrate their commitment to combating AI-generated disinformation in an ethical and responsible manner.

Finally, it is essential for professionals to continuously evaluate and adapt their strategies for combating AI-generated misinformation. As the tactics used by malicious actors continue to evolve, professionals must remain agile and flexible in their approach to detecting and mitigating misinformation. By regularly assessing the effectiveness of their efforts and making necessary adjustments, professionals can stay ahead of the curve and effectively combat the spread of AI-generated disinformation in today's digital landscape.

www.ingramcontent.com/pod-product-compliance
Lightning Source LLC
Chambersburg PA
CBHW082242220526
45479CB00005B/1317